This journal is dedicated to the memory of a wonderful Pet

Place the portrait
of your Pet here

How I first met my Pet
(write a story).

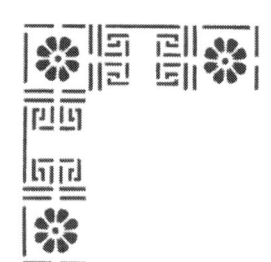

What things about my Pet I liked the most?

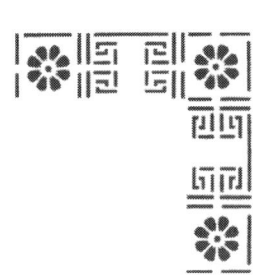

My Pet's favorite things to do.

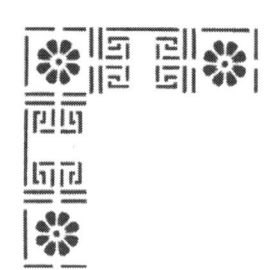

Things I liked to do with my Pet.

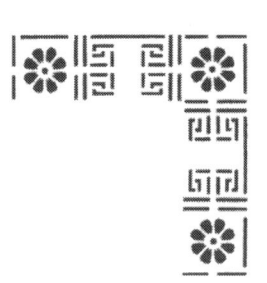

My Pet's favorite
food and treats.

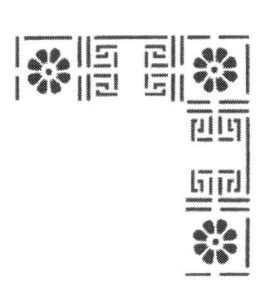

The funniest and silliest
things my Pet
ever did.

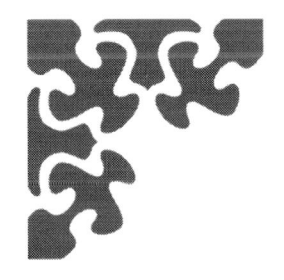

The naughtiest things my Pet ever did.

Why my Pet was
so different from
all the other pets.

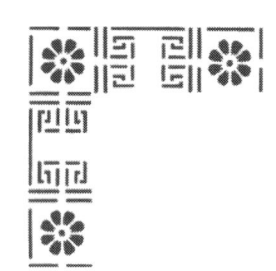

My Pet loved me
and wouldn't want me
to be sad forever.

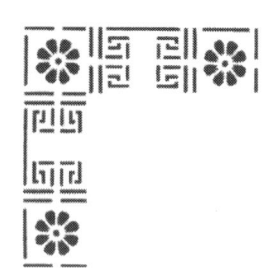

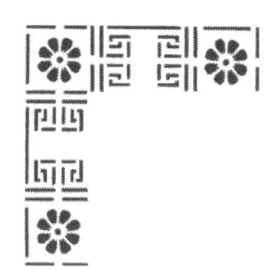

Manufactured by Amazon.ca
Bolton, ON